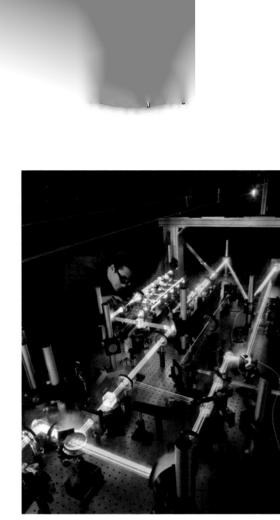

An air force technician
tests a laser.

Laser
Man

Theodore H. Maiman
and His
Brilliant Invention

Edwin Brit Wyckoff

Enslow Elementary
an imprint of
Enslow Publishers, Inc.
40 Industrial Road
Box 398
Berkeley Heights, NJ 07922
USA
        http://www.enslow.com

Content Adviser
Andrew H. Rawicz
Professor of Engineering
Simon Fraser University
Vancouver, Canada

Series Literacy Consultant
Allan A. De Fina, Ph.D.
Past President of the New Jersey Reading Association
Professor, Department of Literacy Education
New Jersey City University

Acknowledgment

The publisher thanks Theodore and Kathleen Maiman for providing many helpful suggestions and photos for the publication of this book.

Library of Congress Cataloging-in-Publication Data

Wyckoff, Edwin Brit.

    Laser man : Theodore H. Maiman and his brilliant invention / by Edwin Brit Wyckoff.

      p. cm. — (Genius at work! Great inventor biographies)

    Includes bibliographical references and index.

    ISBN-13: 978-0-7660-2848-7

    ISBN-10: 0-7660-2848-8

    1. Maiman, Theodore H.—Juvenile literature. 2. Engineers—United States—Biography—Juvenile literature.

      3. Lasers—History—Juvenile literature. I. Title.

    TA140.M2722W93 2007

    621.36'6092—dc22

      [B]

                                             2006034680

Printed in the United States of America

10 9 8 7 6 5 4 3 2 1

To Our Readers

We have done our best to make sure all Internet addresses in this book were active and appropriate when we went to press. However, the author and the publisher have no control over and assume no liability for the material available on those Internet sites or on other Web sites they may link to. Any comments or suggestions can be sent by e-mail to comments@enslow.com or to the address on the back cover.

Every effort has been made to locate all copyright holders of material used in this book. If any errors or omissions have occurred, corrections will be made in future editions of this book.

Photo Credits: AIP Emilio Segrè Visual Archives, Hecht Collection, p. 17; courtesy Air Force Research Laboratory's Directed Energy Directorate, pp. 1 (top), 3 (top inset); Homer and Jean Hill, p. 9; courtesy of HRL Laboratories, LLC., pp. 3 (background), 18, 19, 21; courtesy Robin M. Izzo, p. 6 (both); courtesy Kathleen Maiman, pp. 7, 8, 12, 20, 22, 23, 24, 28; courtesy of the Maiman Family, p. 10; NASA/JPL, p. 4; National Archives and Records Administration, courtesy AIP Emilio Segrè Visual Archives, p. 16; © Charles O'Rear/CORBIS, p. 25; Sam Ogden/Photo Researchers, Inc., p. 26; Shutterstock, p. 14 (all); courtesy University of Colorado Alumni Association (photo has been color-enhanced), pp. 1 (bottom), 3 (bottom inset)

Cover Photo: Courtesy Air Force Research Laboratory's Directed Energy Directorate (background); courtesy University of Colorado Alumni Association (inset, photo has been color-enhanced)

Contents

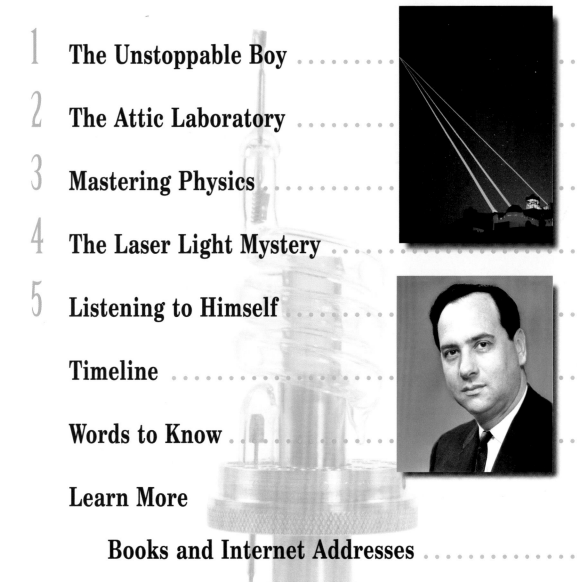

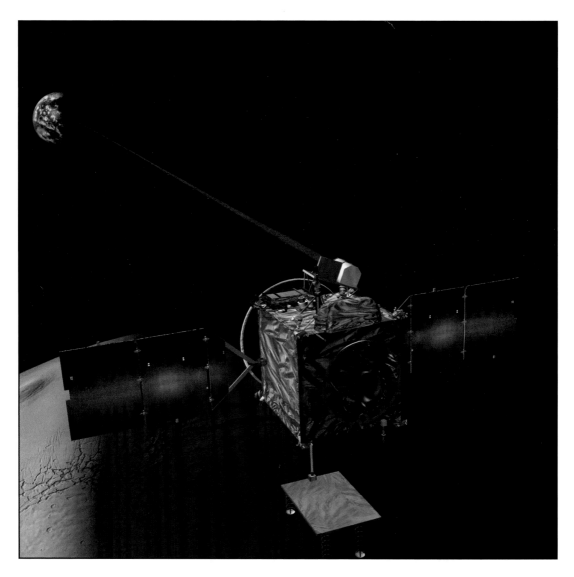

This picture was created by a computer. It shows how
a beam of light could travel from Earth to a spacecraft.
In space, the beam would be invisible.

Chapter 1

The Unstoppable Boy

A very narrow beam of light was sent racing into the sky from the United States in 2005. It was testing contact between Earth and *MESSENGER*, a U.S. spacecraft exploring other planets. The narrow rays of light were aimed at a six-inch mirror on the spacecraft. They bounced back 15 million miles to Earth at blazing speeds. Amazingly, the beam of light came from a small lamp. That lamp was no stronger than the light bulb inside an ordinary oven in an ordinary home. It was not movie magic. It was a laser.

Lasers make very narrow, very bright beams of light. Today there are many kinds of lasers made from many different materials. Doctors can use one kind of laser like a knife to operate

Light from a light bulb spreads in every direction. It is very hard to read with only a ten-watt bulb.

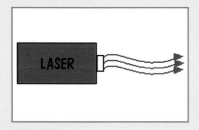

Light from a ten-watt laser is very narrow, very concentrated, and very powerful. To make a laser, light is bounced back and forth inside a material, such as a ruby. With each bounce, the light gets stronger until it escapes out one side as a laser beam.

on human eyes. Other kinds of laser beams are so strong they can cut through thick steel.

During the 1950s, many scientists worked on the idea of lasers. Yet none knew how to make laser light. Ted Maiman thought he had found a way. But almost every scientist he talked to said that his idea would not work. Ted did not listen. He would not give up trying to build his laser.

Theodore Harold Maiman was born in

Los Angeles, California, on July 11, 1927. The next year, he moved to Denver, Colorado with his parents, Abe and Rose Ann, and his sister, Estelle. They lived together with Ted's grandparents, aunts, uncles, and cousins.

Ted wanted to know how everything worked. His family had great patience as he took apart every machine he could get his hands on.

When he was three, Ted said that the light in the refrigerator stayed on even when the door was closed. His mother did not believe him at first. But when they checked, they saw that the light stayed on all the time because the switch was not working. His mother then had the light switch fixed.

Another time, Ted felt that all his aunt's lipsticks, creams, and face powder were really for mixing up into

Ted and his sister, Estelle

great new colors. Even a loving aunt did not think that was funny.

Ted was curious and full of energy. He became the class clown, making all his classmates laugh. One teacher tried to calm him down. She gave him special math problems to solve. He liked that.

Ted with his parents, Abe and Rose Ann

When he was twelve, Ted got a job in a shop fixing broken radios. The next year, his boss decided to work in a factory making equipment for soldiers. He surprised Ted by offering to let him run the shop all by himself. Ted took charge.

In high school, Ted enjoyed his busy life. He went to clarinet practice with the school band at seven in the morning. After school, he rushed downtown to his job in an electrical repair shop. Then he raced back home

Ted moved to Morristown, New Jersey, when he was sixteen.

for dinner. Afterward, Ted hurried back downtown to the University of Colorado. There he was allowed to take a free class on how radios work, even though he was still too young for college.

In 1943, his family moved to Morristown, New Jersey. This ended his career as a radio repairman.

As a teen, Ted learned much about electronics.

Chapter 2

The Attic Laboratory

Ted's father, Abe, was an inventor who helped find a way for radios to work in cars. He also invented a new tool that let doctors hear a human heartbeat much more clearly. Abe put together a laboratory in the attic of their home in Morristown. At night and on weekends, he worked on his inventions. Ted watched and listened.

Abe hoped that Ted would grow up to make things that would help doctors save lives. Soon, Ted began trying his own experiments.

Ted built a strong magnet powered by electricity. He set it up right next to one of his father's delicate scientific tools. When he turned on the magnet, it tore his father's tool to pieces.

Ted in his navy uniform

Abe said nothing, but for years Ted still felt bad about breaking his father's tool.

Ted was in high school when he got a job moving heavy machinery in a factory. The work was backbreaking. The pay was sixty cents an hour. He asked for a different job. He wanted to work with electrical wires, a job that paid ninety cents an hour. The owners said no to the sixteen-year-old. Even so, Ted never stopped asking for better jobs. One year later, he got a new job building radio parts for the military. World War II, which began in 1939, was raging across Europe and Asia.

Ted turned seventeen in 1944 and joined the United States Navy. There he would create tools to test radar. Radar uses radio waves to find enemy boats and airplanes.

Engineers use math and physics to design and build new things like cars, computers, airplanes, cameras, and musical instruments.

Chapter  3

Mastering Physics

After serving in the navy, Ted entered the University of Colorado to study science. In 1949, he graduated with a degree in engineering physics. His heart was set on continuing his study of physics. Physics would help him understand computers, television, and even ideas about lasers. Stanford University in California, where he wanted to go, did not accept him. So he traveled to New York City to study physics at Columbia University.

But Ted was stubborn. He applied to Stanford University again and again. He was sure it would be the best school for him. The university said no every time. Then he asked to study engineering instead of physics. This time, he was told yes. In 1951, he earned a master's degree in electrical engineering. With this degree, and after years of being told no, Ted was finally allowed to study advanced physics at Stanford.

At the university, Ted worked as a laboratory assistant for Dr. Willis Lamb. Ted's work was so good that Dr. Lamb wanted Ted to stay longer and longer. But Ted wanted to finish his studies and move on with his own work.

Dr. Willis Lamb won the Nobel Prize in Physics in 1955. The Nobel Prize is one of the world's highest honors for a scientist.

Ted made a deal with Dr. Lamb. Before he would leave Stanford, Ted would train a bright young man named Irwin Wieder to take over his job. Wieder would later play a

Irwin Wieder (right) learned many of the same ideas about physics as Ted in Dr. Lamb's laboratory.

part in the story of the first laser. Ted earned the highest college degree, his Ph.D., in physics in 1955.

Free at last, it was time for a vacation. Ted wanted to travel. He bought a ticket for a boat trip around the world. He had gone only halfway when he decided the vacation was over. He was eager to start working. He flew back home on the first flight he could get. In January 1956, Ted quickly found a job at the Hughes Research Laboratory in Culver City, California.

The Hughes Research Laboratory is known as HRL Laboratories today. This picture shows the lab in Malibu, California. It moved there in 1960.

Ted settled down and married Shirley Rich that year. In 1958 their daughter, Sheri, was born. Life on the California coast was pleasant, but soon it would all change.

The Laser Light Mystery

In 1959, Hughes Research Laboratory put Ted in charge of a project to build a laser. Many scientists said that it could not be done. Other scientists said that a laser would not do anything useful. Ted just closed his ears and began working on lasers.

Ted with one of his lasers

He was given $50,000 by the Hughes Research Laboratory to pay for one assistant and to buy equipment. That sounds like a lot of money. It was not. Research teams at other companies had hundreds of scientists and millions of dollars to spend. The lasers those teams wanted to build were huge. Such lasers also had to be cooled way down below freezing.

Ted had different ideas about his laser. First, he wanted his laser to work above freezing. Second, his laser had to be small enough to hold in his hand. Nobody could change Ted's mind, because he wanted his laser to be easy to use.

Ted's first laser was small enough to hold in his hand.

Ted had some dark red rubies left over from his early experiments at Stanford University. But sending beams of light through them did not work very well. Next, he used a pink ruby. He tried and tried to make laser light. Still nothing happened.

Most other laser scientists thought Ted's idea would not work. But Ted was never willing to take anything for granted. Just because some famous scientists thought rubies would not work, they did not convince him.

Then the young scientist Ted had trained at Stanford, Irwin Wieder, did tests on pink rubies. The tests showed they would never make laser light. Ted would not listen to other scientists, but because he had trained Wieder himself, Ted believed him. Racing against

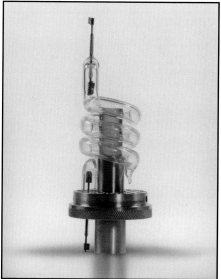

The first laser

21

other laser scientists, Ted gave up on the ruby and tried using many other kinds of materials.

The $50,000 began to drain away. Ted put in long hours at the laboratory. He took work home, just as his father had done. This did not make Shirley happy. She and Ted later divorced.

Ted's experiments were not working, but he did not give up. He decided to check Wieder's tests. This time, the tests showed the ruby could make laser light. Wieder and all the other scientists had been wrong. Even the smartest people do make mistakes.

Ted turned back to the pink ruby. He ordered a new one about the size of a sugar cube. He sent away

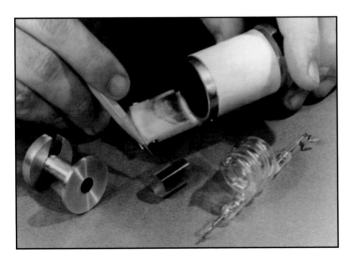

This is the pink ruby and the lamp used in the first laser.

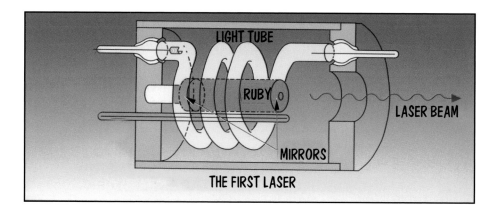

This drawing shows how the first laser worked. When the light tube was lit up, light bounced back and forth inside the ruby. As it bounced, it got stronger until it escaped as a laser beam.

for a photographic lamp that sent out sharp, powerful flashes of light. Waiting for the ruby and the lamp to be shipped to him seemed to take forever. It was April 1960. Eight months had passed since he started his research, and there was still no laser. Most of the money had been spent.

The next month, the special lamp and the new pink ruby arrived. Ted and his assistant put together an instrument that could be held in one hand. They turned on the power. A very narrow, brilliant light burned through the air. The laser light mystery had been solved. Ted Maiman had built the first laser.

Ted holds the first laser. Behind him is the much larger Nova laser at the Lawrence Livermore National Laboratory in Livermore, California.

An important science writer called Ted's laser a fake. Newspaper headlines shouted that a "death ray" had been invented. That was silly. Angry scientists said again and again that Ted's laser could not do anything. They would be proved wrong. Ted knew he had created something useful.

Listening to Himself

Many people spend their lives playing follow the leader. Even scientists may be afraid to break the rules laid down years before by somebody famous. The rules for a laser that most scientists were following never included a small pink ruby. That may be why it took so long to build the first laser.

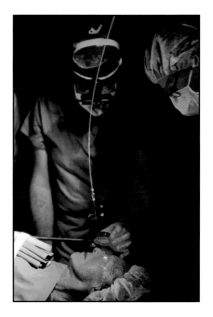

Lasers today can be used in eye surgery.

Inventors like Ted Maiman go to work every day trying to make their ideas work, but many things do not work right the first time. They stay awake at night trying to figure out how to fix what went wrong. It is like trying to finish a jigsaw puzzle without a picture to use as a guide. Many people give up just before they could have put the whole puzzle together. One extra drop of courage keeps inventors going when everyone else has given up.

Abe Maiman lived to see his son win science prizes from all around the world for his fantastic invention. He remembered spending time with

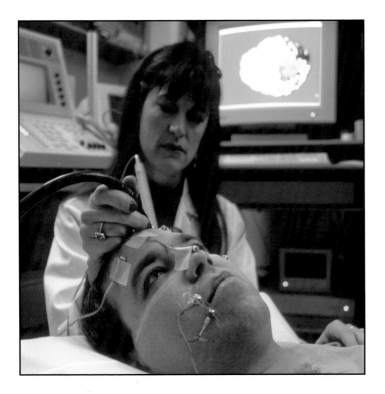

A laser helps to map this man's brain.

young Ted in his attic laboratory. Abe had wanted his son to use physics and engineering to help doctors help people. Abe saw his dream become real. His son's lasers are used by doctors for difficult surgery. Today, lasers repair thousands of human eyes every year. They can help to destroy cancer in many patients. Ted was invited to join the Royal College of Surgeons of England because his lasers were great new tools for doctors.

Lasers Can Do Fantastic Things

The brilliant light from lasers can be sharper than a knife and hotter than a blowtorch. These are just a few things lasers can do:

Perform delicate eye surgery

Remove tattoos

Erase birthmarks

Help surgeons operate without causing bleeding

Cut steel and other metals

Weld metal together

Burn holes in diamonds

Read CDs and DVDs

Send phone calls through a fiberglass strand thinner than human hair

Measure the distance from the Earth to the Moon

Guide airplanes and spacecraft

Read price barcodes with a supermarket scanner

Create fabulous light shows for theaters and concerts

In 1984, Ted was voted into America's National Inventor's Hall of Fame. Awards kept pouring in as new uses for lasers were discovered. He married again. He and his wife, Kathleen, lived in Vancouver, Canada, until his death in May 2007.

Ted Maiman had the extra drop of courage to listen to himself when everyone else told him he was wrong. He had the wonderful memory of having been right all along. Ted's laser has made many once impossible things possible in our world today.

Ted received the Japan Prize in 1987. His wife, Kathleen, shakes hands with Emperor Akihito of Japan as Ted looks on.

1927 Born in Los Angeles, California, on July 11.

1928 Family moves to Denver, Colorado.

1939 Becomes assistant in one-man radio shop.

1943 Family moves to Morristown, New Jersey.

1944 Joins navy; creates testing tools for radar.

1949 Graduates with bachelor of science in engineering physics from the University of Colorado.

1951 Earns master of science degree in engineering from Stanford University, California.

1955 Earns Ph.D. in physics from Stanford University.

1956 Marries Shirley Rich; joins Hughes Research Laboratory, in Culver City, California.

1958 Daughter Sheri is born.

1960 Demonstrates the world's first laser on May 16.

1962 Founds Korad Company to produce ruby lasers.

1969 Gets divorced from Shirley.

1984 Is elected to National Inventor's Hall of Fame; meets and marries Kathleen Heath; moves to Vancouver, Canada.

2007 Dies in Vancouver on May 5.

engineering—Using math and physics to design and build new things.

laboratory—A place to do scientific experiments.

laser—An instrument that makes a very narrow and very strong beam of light. Lasers can be used to cut hard material, remove diseased body tissue, and more.

Ph.D.—The highest degree a student can earn from a university. It means doctor of philosophy.

physics—The science of materials and energy and how they act together.

radar—Radio waves used to find objects. Radar is used by the military to find enemy boats and airplanes.

ruby—A precious pink or red natural stone often used in jewelry. Rubies can also be made in laboratories and used for science.

university—A place where people go to learn after graduating from high school.

watt—In physics, a unit to measure how powerful something is.

Books

Clements, Gillian. *The Picture History of Great Inventors*. London: Frances Lincoln, 2005.

Macaulay, David. *The New Way Things Work*. Boston: Houghton Mifflin Co., 1998.

Sadler, Wendy. *Light: Look Out!* Chicago: Raintree, 2006.

Internet Addresses

NASA Space Place
http://spaceplace.nasa.gov/en/kids/laser/index.shtml

Optics for Kids
http://www.opticalres.com/kidoptx_f.html